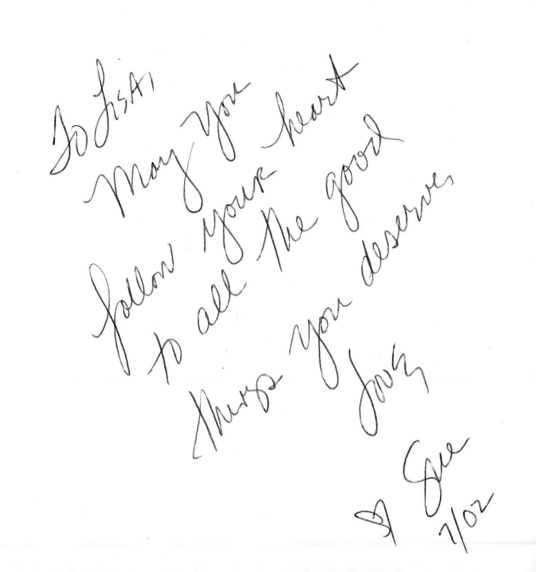

To Lisa,

May you
follow your heart
to all the good
things you deserve

Love
Sue
♡ 7/02

the woman who lost her heart

A Tale of Reawakening

Innisfree
Press, Inc.
A call to the
deep heart's core

susan o'halloran
susan delattre

Innisfree Press, Inc.
136 Roumfort Road
Philadelphia, PA 19119-1632

Library of Congress Cataloging-in-Publication Data
O'Halloran, Susan.
    The woman who lost her heart : a tale of reawakening / by Susan
O'Halloran and Susan Delattre.
        p.   cm.
    ISBN 1-880913-27-5
    I. Delattre, Susan, date.   II. Title.
PS3565.H27W6   1997
813'.54—dc20   92-8661
                                CIP

The Woman Who Lost Her Heart

To two of my best friends, my sons, Terry and Preston Luke

ACKNOWLEDGMENTS

I would like to thank: skilled professionals and friends such as Karan Turnblom, Ron Morris, Bali sisters, The Thursday Group, the Creative Life gang in Milwaukee, and especially Betty Erb and Jim Morningstar for introducing me to the young one within and the power of my own breath. Mary and Kathy McHugh and the Hallorans—Michael, MaryBarb, Katie, Tom, and Mike—for physical support of all kinds. The Loft and Minnesota writer colleagues for encouraging me to write. My dear Chicago and Twin Cities friends for their personal support and marketing help, especially Tess Galati, Axel Anderson, Karen Kolberg for sharing their knowledge. My adoptive parents, Jerry and Marilyn Sexton, and my adopted sister, Krysta Kavenaugh, for teaching the ways of unconditional love. And to Krysta's Playfair bunch out of Berkeley for their encouragement as Susan and I finished this book at the "Nerds In Paradise Retreat" in Florida. And, most of all to Susan Delattre, my friend, confidante, and storytelling partner. She is one of the most supportive, accepting people on the planet. She has taught me that creation is easy and work a joy.

— SUE O'HALLORAN

In memory of my mother, Clara

ACKNOWLEDGMENTS

I want to acknowledge those who have been close companions during the time in which this book was written: Fran Ouellette, for her beautifully sensitive readings of the Tarot; Ric Watson, who taught me to feel the bones in my feet; Fran Kaliher, for sharing the beauty of her north woods home; my sangha sisters and brothers in the Twin City Vipassana Cooperative; all those who walked with me that early June morning in the Lake Harriet Rock Garden to honor the passing of my mother; the Full Moon women; Ron, Christopher, and Nancy, my non-nuclear family; Hämsá Hanzak, whose music has opened my being; Ellen Heck, performing partner and friend of many lifetimes; and Diane Elliot, Margie Fargnoli, Rebecca Frost, and Erika Thorne of the Women's Performance Project, who have witnessed my healing and taught me how to let the love in. And of course, Sue O'Halloran, who wants to listen to my stories and be my friend.

— SUSAN DELATTRE

INTRODUCTION

I used to do my life differently. I thought about my career goals when I was twenty, for example, in a logical, list-making kind of way. I'd say, "I want to be in that dance company. Therefore, I need to study modern, ballet, tai chi, composition, folk dancing, and contact improvisation, all of it, by this time next year." And so I mastered ways to juggle eating, sewing my leotard, and doing my warm-up exercises while driving a car, befuddled by the strain my goals caused in real life when they had made so much sense on paper.

At twenty-five, a change was forced upon me when a

dance student plowed into me and the resulting fall sent me in and out of surgery for the next few years. I look at that accident as a time of being wrestled to the ground for a nice, long chat with my body.

I learned that the body speaks. I mean literally—ask your body questions and it will answer—in words, pictures, metaphors, sounds, smells, tastes, and felt sensations. A few more injuries and emotional traumas later and I finally emerged in the fourth decade of my life with a self. It seems absurd that I had lived, loved, and even been competent for thirty-some years without an inner identity, but there you have it. However imperfectly, I was finally living my life from the inside out.

The second miracle—as radical as the discovery that I *had* an inner life—was finding out that others already knew of its existence. While I was growing up, the only clue that there were stirrings of life below the neckline was when I heard a friend of my mother's described as "blue," as in, "She's blue; she has a bad case of nerves." The tone was indisputable—the lady was losing her grip. To feel was to be slightly crazy. Then, in a happy accident, I stumbled upon Joseph Campbell's *The Hero with a Thousand Faces*. Reading the myths showed me that, long before New Age or therapeutic jargon, the inner terrain had already been charted. You could actually talk about the inner world!

At many points in my metamorphosis from a list-driven to an inner-directed life, I felt as though I were being asked to fall voluntarily backward from a Grand Canyon-sized cliff. But during my free fall, the stories rode with me, whispering in my ear, handing me a map, telling me how it was going to be. I wept with relief. I was not crazy; others had done this before me.

We adults need stories as much as children. For me, the greatest joy in performing stories is watching adults turn into three-year-olds. Our eyes grow larger. We snuggle in closer to friends. We hug our own knees. Together we become magicians—a thousand pictures floating around the room —agreeing for that moment to create a space that allows us to feel and encourages us to be.

These days, time has become fluid, sensual, no longer linear. I am continually amazed that when I follow my body's agenda—cry, produce, play, take a nap, talk to a friend—most things do get done and what is unimportant falls away. It's not that I don't make lists anymore, but that I am ready, at the moment and against all logic, to drop any plan the head can devise if it doesn't feel right.

My body's intuition is the check. I follow what it is drawn to and move away from what it shirks. The route I follow is often circuitous, fuzzy, with ill-defined borders, and yet I don't feel spacey or ill-defined myself. The solidity comes not in knowing or controlling the grand design but in sensing that, as I ride the rolling swell, I am being taken care of. If you had told me at twenty that this is how I'd make decisions or plan my life, I would have told you that was impossible. But then I wouldn't have known what you were talking about.

So I offer this book in deep gratitude at having found ways to let go, be guided, and live the heart's truer desires, and in celebration that there are ways to describe our inner journeys and show each other the way. I hope *The Woman Who*

Lost Her Heart encourages you to tell your own stories of change—anecdotally to friends or in more formal ways.

We need each other's stories to remember who we are. When we feel the warmth of our stories, the frozen blocks melt away. It is at those soft places that we finally and joyfully connect. Delight, safety, movement, imagination—they lead us to loving ourselves, our lives, and each other just a little bit more.

— SUE O'HALLORAN

A good story lets me discover something I once knew but have forgotten. Those somethings were once so important that I saved them. I'll need that again, I might have said, or, I'll always want to remember this. But like those old photographs that I put away so carefully in my storage chest, the things I want to remember can sometimes go for years without seeing the light of day. And then a story reminds me.

A good story exercises my imagination. It expands my perception of what is real. I love the elements of fantasy, fairy tale, and myth because they take me out of my narrow sense of how things are and into the Big Story, into the far realms of human being.

A good story resonates in the body. Trained for years as a dancer, I thought I knew my body well. But the gift of the body as a place of learning came only when, with the help of other seekers, I asked my body for the stories. With help, with patience, and with tenderness I listen now to what the body knows, to what the cells themselves want to forget and what they want to remember.

A good story shows me how I'm the same and how I'm different from others and helps me to celebrate both. Stories give me a marvelous sense of what it means to be a human being. In that way, we humans create ourselves together by sharing our stories.

The Woman Who Lost Her Heart began as a story told out

loud, in a rehearsal studio, as Sue and I prepared to share an evening of storytelling. That was years ago. We didn't know then that our collaboration would grow into a book. We just knew the story tugged on us both. It reminded us of what we had forgotten. It asked us to share in its creation, same and different as we are. It is a story we imagined together, a story we re-membered from the body. It comes to you now in written form to be part of the Big Story, the one all of us are creating together.

— SUSAN DELATTRE

The Woman Who Lost Her Heart

CHAPTER ONE

 nce upon these times, in a future not too distant from our own, a woman awoke to find she had lost her heart. It simply wasn't inside her. In a panic the woman searched everywhere. With all the beiges and browns in her house, a heart should have stood out, easy to be seen. But her heart was nowhere to be found.

"This can't be," the woman said. "Tomorrow's our Face-to-Face. Our first Face-to-Face meeting in three years.

I can't miss that."

She put her hand on her chest but could not feel her own pulse. Prior to that morning's disappearance, she had always had plenty of heart, enough blood pumping to keep her racing from morning until night. Since she had been a little girl, she had wanted only one thing—to be the best at whatever she did, to be able to turn back at a late age and point to a body of work and say, "I did that and it was good."

To that end, she had worked at many different jobs where she was constantly busy trying to do more so that she could get noticed. But oddly enough, the more she did, the more she found herself wondering if she was actually accomplishing anything. Even though she was overwhelmed, she kept saying "yes" to more assignments because she never knew for sure if she was doing enough.

It was the time when most office buildings were obsolete. Co-workers communicated from their homes through their computers or fax machines, rarely in person. That's why it was hard for the woman to know for sure if her bosses were pleased with her work. The evaluations were good, but reading about one's performance on a computer printout was not the same as a pat on the back. Just the month before she had gone to the Satellite Conference Center to have a video interview with her mentor, a wise and powerful woman who seemed to know everything. The woman wanted to talk about this constant, gnawing feeling—too many last minute details, never enough last minutes.

"Never time to do things right, but always time to do them over?" her mentor had asked.

"That's it," the woman had answered. "And doing

them over means working weekends and lots of overtime during the week. I know there are other things I should be doing, but I've worked hard for my new position. I don't want to wreck it now."

"What do you do for yourself? When do *you* take a break?"

"Oh, I take a coffee break each day . . . usually at lunch . . ."

"Listen to you," her mentor had scoffed. "You're drinking coffee to slow down."

The woman had laughed at herself, remembering that the week before at dinner she had said to a friend, "I think I just swallowed that Salisbury steak whole." Her friend had laughed, for the woman was known for her singular sense of humor. "No, I'm not kidding. I think I've forgotten how to chew. Remember when we were kids and we'd take five minutes to eat one piece of candy and we'd taste every bit of it? I don't taste my food anymore. I do everything in a hurry."

Her friend had responded, "Welcome to the real world."

"Is this what life's about?" the woman had asked her mentor. "I thought this is what I wanted, but I'm so busy making my reports sound good that I don't even know sometimes what actually happened. I bring my portable computer with me on vacation. It's like I'm not even there. I feel as if I've accomplished something when I save five seconds by running up an escalator. I make phone calls, balance my checkbook, and eat lunch while I drive.

"Yesterday when I took my niece to a museum, I got so frustrated with how slowly she was moving I yelled, 'Come on! Keep walking. If you stop to look at everything, you won't *see* anything!' Can you believe it? I was scolding my niece for enjoying herself. This has got to stop," the woman had complained to her mentor. "What's happening to me?"

"What *is* happening to you?" her mentor had asked.

"I don't know. I went to a goal-setting seminar, but by the time I left I had twelve new goals including finding time for time management classes. The wall-size 'Schedule of the Week' in my office looks like military strategy for a full year. I decided to hire someone to help with housework, and I spent an hour making sure the house was clean before she arrived. I took an exercise class in speed walking, and now I've gotten compulsive about taking the perfect walk. Maybe now is not the right time to change old habits. When the new format comes out—then I'll take a break."

The woman worked for a holographic movie company. She was producer/director of three-dimensional travelogues. Thanks to her company, families could walk through the sights and sounds of France, Mexico, Bali, or Greece right in their own living rooms. But no sooner had her company come out with the 3-D format, then ten other companies did the same. Now her company was on the verge of surpassing all the competition put together. They were just a hair's breadth away from perfecting the Adventure Simulator Capsule (ASC), a complete home environmental experience. Not only would those who entered the ASC roll, soar, pitch, and plunge through 3-D images, they would also smell the Holland flowers, feel the Sahara heat, drip in the Caribbean humidity, and shiver in the Iceland snow. Those who wanted to go to the Arctic would have to *dress* for the Arctic when they used the

Adventure Simulator Capsule.

That's why this upcoming meeting was so important. The company could not chance an electronic leak about their new environmental box. Hence the Face-to-Face meeting, the first in three years, to plan the announcement of the Adventure Simulator Capsule.

"If I can't find my heart, I can't make it to this meeting," the woman thought. "And if I can't make it to this meeting, I'll be back marketing holographic mannequins for department store windows. Blow a 3-D kiss and sell the latest fashions. Oh, I can't do that again."

The woman was desperate. She called Central Control. "Hi. Is the Face-to-Face still on for tomorrow? Did the Benson contract get approved? Is my crew scheduled for the Stonehenge location?" And then she added, "Oh, yeah, by the way, I seem to have lost my heart." The woman looked down and saw her fingers shaking on top of the control panel.

"Turn on the video for your phone," Central Control requested. Though the woman logged in every morning with Central Control, because it *was* morning, she never flipped on the visual. CC had never seen her, and she had never seen Central.

"Wow! You don't look so hot!" Central Control said.

"Great. What am I going to do?"

"Hey, listen," Central Control said, "since everyone's traveling today to get to the meeting, it's kind of slow here. Why don't we meet for breakfast?"

An hour later at breakfast, Central Control, whose name was Monica, sat across from the woman and stared. "You're sitting here," Monica said to the woman. "You're breathing. How can you be alive if you don't have a heart?"

"I don't know if I am alive," the woman said. "Feel my skin. Go ahead. Touch me." The woman dropped her eyes, bit her lip, and stuck out her arm to Monica. Monica reached toward the woman. She could feel the difference in temperature in the air around the woman, and when she actually touched the woman's arm, it was clammy and cold.

"Wow!" Monica exclaimed. "You can't go to the meeting like this. I don't think it would make a very good first impression."

"But I've got to go. What possible excuse could I give? Even if I say I'm sick, you know they'll just use the videophone. Everyone will still know there's something wrong with me. You did."

Monica's beeper went off, and she excused herself to

read the printout in private. She returned to the table with a big smile on her face. "You're in luck."

"What do you mean? What's going on?"

"There's some bug in the ASC. The top dogs are stopping at the factory before they come here. We're rescheduling the meeting for Thursday. Looks like you have a few more days to find your heart."

"Great!" the woman said. She slipped on her jacket and gave CC a cold squeeze to her hand. "And I know right where I'll start looking."

❖

The woman raced to the Satellite Conference Center to arrange a meeting with her mentor. She sat in front of a large video screen, and when she aimed the remote control at the set, it turned on. There on the screen was her mentor.

"Lost your heart, eh?" the mentor said. "Started looking for it yet?"

"Well, just around the house," the woman answered. "Then I got frustrated and called CC, I mean Central Control."

"What about the things we talked about last time? How has your schedule been?" the mentor asked.

"Busy as usual," the woman answered. "You know we're shooting in a slightly different format for the environmental box I told you about. So actually, we're reshooting almost everything we have plus producing new titles for families who won't have the capsule for another year or two."

The mentor said nothing.

"You know, we always have to double up when there's

a transition to a new format. But this is going to be it, really. After the announcement . . ."

"Do you think that could have anything to do with losing your heart?"

"Oh, I've been using my heart plenty," the woman replied. "I've been running around like a robot with its head cut off."

The mentor did not laugh.

"Okay," the woman said, "Maybe you're right. I have been pushing it, I know. But right now, do I really need to know *why* I lost my heart? Isn't it more important that I figure out how to get it back? Can you tell me?"

The mentor smiled and nodded her head.

"Well?" the woman asked with excited impatience.

"If you want to find your heart again, you will have to

go to the Great Valley."

"Oh, no!" exclaimed the woman. "The Great Valley? I can't go there."

CHAPTER TWO

 he mentor remained quiet, and the woman knew there was little use pleading, but in spite of herself she tried one more time. "Surely there's some other way."

The woman had met other people who had gone to the Great Valley. Some of them had been gone a long time; some of them changed so much that when they finally did return, their own families did not recognize them. And they all talked so strangely. They spoke of "discovering joy by embracing their pain." They spoke of "finding themselves by grieving their losses." The thought of returning like one of them filled the woman with great apprehension.

"I was thinking more along the lines of going to one of the medical centers that have perfected the artificial heart. Not that I like the idea of a plastic ticker, mind you, but . . ."

The mentor's silence was the woman's answer.

"If you want to find your heart," the mentor said, "you will have to spend at least three nights in the Great Valley. Each night you will have a visitor who will bring you a heart. You will have to decide if it is yours. Three visitors—three hearts from which to choose."

"How will I know which heart is mine?" the woman asked.

"You will know because you already know, if you

remember how to know," the mentor answered.

"Oh, swell," the woman thought to herself, "Great Valley doublespeak has already begun."

"But be careful. If the heart the visitor brings you should ever touch you, it will be yours, whether you want it or not."

"This is rare," the woman thought. "I have to learn how to know if the heart is mine, but if I make a mistake, it's all over."

As if the mentor read the woman's thoughts, she added, "There are only three steps to finding your heart. First, be aware and breathe. Second, feel and heal. Third, open and grow."

"Oh well, that sounds easy enough," the woman responded quickly, but in her chest she felt a swelling panic.

She had no idea what her mentor was speaking about.

"Don't worry," the mentor spoke again. "I will loan you my Universal Remote. If you do not like the heart, you can just turn the visitor off before the heart ever touches you. And with this Universal Remote you can turn on anything you need, as you need it."

The woman looked down to see in her lap a brand new remote. It was bigger than any other she had ever seen. It had hundreds of buttons, buttons for things like a solar-powered stretch limo, a $500,000 line of credit to buy a modest starter home, and even a button for Ben & Jerry's Antique Ice Cream.

The mentor spoke in a soft, reassuring voice, "You are never sent on such a journey unless you are ready to go." Then the mentor added, "And remember: You never have to go it alone."

The mentor gestured toward the remote. The woman looked down, and on the remote appeared a button the woman had not noticed before. It read, "Others who have gone to the Great Valley."

"Well," the woman sighed, "I suppose I could talk to others who have made this trip but . . . I don't mean to be rude . . . frankly, the ones I have met talk such mumbo jumbo. I don't understand them. And besides . . ." The woman looked down and saw that her skin was turning an ashy grey. "I've got to get my heart back quickly. We're having a Face-to-Face on Thursday, and I can't look like this—if I'm even alive by then. I've got to hurry."

The woman waved good-bye to her mentor, closed her eyes and pushed the button marked "GV."

❖

"Why it's nothing more than a big, old sand pit," the woman cried. "I'm stuck in a deserted desert! What kind of a joke is this?"

Perhaps the woman had expected to be sent to a valley surrounded by green rolling hills or one of the new, underwater colonies built into deep valley trenches in the ocean floor. A sandy, dry desert was not on her list of priorities. "We filmed the great deserts of the world," the woman whined, "and it was some of the worst shoots I've ever been on."

The Great Valley was particularly rocky and bare. Patches of salt dotted the landscape where ponds had once been. The wind blew columns of sand that rippled like flowing water about the woman. A channel that had once been a river was filled with broken stones washed down from the mountains in the distance. The wind-blown sand whittled the desert rocks into eerie, jagged shapes. Huge dunes crept continuously forward, closing in on her even in this wide-open space. Only one lone ocotillo bush stood out green against the shifting carpet of hot, white sand.

The woman had absolutely no idea what to do with herself. First she imagined that she was on a shoot. "Mario, how about starting with a low angle on the rocks? Latoya, circle the bush over there." Often when she had been working, she would imagine how she looked from the outside as if one of the cameras were following her. She had the image just right; her posture was strong, her tone of voice resonant and low, her hand gestures confident, slicing through the air, making her point. And even when Central Control gave her impossible schedules—five different locations in one day—she never missed a deadline. Even when she felt she might cry from exhaustion, she could direct her workers like a team of wild horses, pulling the strays in, keeping crew and equipment all racing in the same direction at exhilarating speeds. The woman stared at her desert surroundings. "Why, we would have been in and out of here in twenty minutes," the woman thought to herself with pride. But here she was, still in the Great Valley desert alone.

Her throat was dry and scratchy. The woman wandered about for a while, but her eyes found little to focus on to distract her restlessness. Then she realized the tickle in her throat was thirst. "Got to find some water," she whispered as though not to scare herself. The riverbed was definitely dry. She seemed to remember reading something as a child about cacti holding water, but cacti also had prickly spines to protect their supply. A desert tortoise looked at the woman for a moment, then ducked its head back under its shell to get out of the sun.

"I wish I had your protection," she said to the tortoise, then shrieked, "Oh, the remote! I completely forgot about it!" The woman ran to her traveling bag, but when she pulled out the remote, all the buttons had disappeared except one. It read, "Fear."

"What is this? I need water!" the woman screamed at the remote.

The Fear button blinked faster. Then other buttons lit up labeled with similar words: "Terrified," "Anxious," "Petrified," "Scared."

"A lot of good this does me!" the woman cried and flung the remote onto the desert floor. "I've got to try and get to those mountains. There's bound to be some water up there and something I can eat."

She began to remove layers of clothing. For a moment she felt cooler, but soon the relentless sun made her flesh hotter than it was before. That was the difference from when she had been in the desert for the film shoot. When she was making her movie, she hadn't felt the desert. Sure, she knew it was hot, but her mind was occupied with keeping on time and on budget, and she did not register the temperature. Now as she made her way to the mountain, every pore of her body seemed to soak in the heat. The heat made its way into the center of her being. If she could have touched her bones, the woman was sure they would be as hot as molten steel. Across a mosaic of cracked, dry earth, the woman placed one inflamed foot in front of the other. Her shoes were stinging, fiery hot, but the woman did not dare take them off. She laughed as she thought of all the money her company was spending to simulate the desert's heat.

"It's all right here for free!" she yelled to no one, as she threw up her arms and turned in circles. "I'm experiencing the real thing, and it hasn't cost me a cent!" She grabbed hold of her arms and hugged them in front of her. "Oh dear," she thought when she realized she'd been talking to herself and laughing out loud, "I'm losing my mind."

And then the woman hoped that she *was* losing her mind. She wished that what she was seeing was some kind of mirage. After hours of walking, the woman found herself back at the ocotillo bush. She knew it was the same bush because there was her jacket, snagged on the bottom stalk.

"Oh no," she said and fell to her knees. "I've been walking in a circle!" The inside of the woman's throat felt as dry as scorched paper. Her limbs were so weak they could not obey her command to walk to the bush. Instead, she crawled. As she reached for her clothing to cover her burned and blistered skin, all the leaves from the ocotillo bush dropped to the ground. At that moment, worse than the thought that she was dying of thirst, the sight of those green leaves on the ground brought on uncontrollable sobs. She knew the leaves would turn brown soon, and all the color in the desert would be gone. She gathered a fistful of leaves in her hand and pressed them to her cheek. A moment of coolness trickled across her face, and her tears turned to tears of gratitude.

Then she remembered and exclaimed, "The remote! Maybe it has new buttons on it!" The woman sat up and looked in every direction. She did not see the remote, but she did spot a new, small dune forming to her left. The woman crawled to the new sandpile and began digging. Hurriedly, she scooped out double handfuls of sand and then, a few inches down, she found the remote. She grabbed it with both hands and furiously wiped the sand from its facing. Still the word "Fear" blinked up at her.

"Okay, I'm afraid!" the woman sobbed and pushed the button. "And I'm sad, too! All right? So what?"

A spiral of sand swirled around the woman. All at once the woman realized it was not dying she was sad about; she was weeping for her life, a life she would dearly miss. She wanted more than a button marked "Water." She wanted buttons for the smell of freshly cut grass and the sight of a sky full of stars. Sitting in that wind-blown sand, she remembered the smell of lilac bushes in spring and the feel of endless summer days and the sight of deep golden light inside houses on cold winter nights. She remembered when she was five and she first became aware of her own skin as cool air skidded across her flesh right before a thunderstorm. It was better than any of the movies she ever shot, better than any environmental capsule her company would invent because it was real and she had felt it. She had felt all those things right as they happened. And she wanted to live to feel more things again.

"Oh, God, I want to stay on this planet!" the woman cried and made herself laugh from the strange sound of those words. She had not thought of living as a choice; it was something she had always taken for granted. And then she heard an even stranger sound—a voice coming from deep within her. "You are enough," the voice said. "You have enough. You are always taken care of."

"Oh, dear, I *am* going crazy," the woman thought. She

wiped the tears from her eyes. The remote in her hand was soaked. "Maybe I can drink my tears," she laughed grimly again, then glimpsed something new on the remote. She blinked the tears from her eyes and read the word, "Rain."

"Rain!" she squealed. "Rain!" The woman pushed the button and leapt to her feet just as the first thunderclouds appeared. Thunder rumbled and boomed, and lightning pierced the green underside of clouds. Torrents of white-capped muddy water raced down from the mountains and filled the stone-laden channel within minutes. The ocotillo bush sprouted tender blossoms of red.

The woman spent the rest of the day floating in the stream, taking drinks of water when she wanted, doing nothing, thinking nothing, just staring at the sky. When the sun began to sink, a moist coolness moved across her body, as luscious as biting into a perfectly ripe orange.

"An orange," she thought. "Maybe the Universal Remote will have a button for an orange." But when she got out of the stream and picked up the remote, only three buttons blinked: "Pillow," "Blanket," and "Towel." She felt a flash of anger zip through her body. "What happened to the Ben & Jerry's ice cream?"

Then she remembered her mentor's words: "With this Universal Remote you can turn on anything you need—as you need it." The woman pressed the button marked "Towel" and dried off her body, then requested a pillow and blanket. "I guess for right now this is all I need," the woman sighed, lay down, and drifted toward sleep.

She was almost asleep when she heard a sound. At first she thought she was dreaming, caught between that land of waking and sleeping. But no, she definitely heard a sound. The squeaking scrunch of someone walking on the cold night sand. *Scrunch. Scrunch. Scrunch. Scrunch.* The footsteps came closer and closer.

CHAPTER THREE

man appeared before her. Standing in the moonlight, dressed in riding jodhpurs and wearing high leather boots, the man carried a riding crop in one hand, and in the other he held a huge heart—a heart! It was glistening, alive, and beating in his hand.

"This heart comes from my finest stallion," the man said. "It could be yours. These days it's nothing to put in a new heart. With a heart like this, you'll run like the wind. No one will be able to outlast you. And people will come from everywhere to watch you. With a heart like this, no one will be more famous, more powerful, more accomplished than you."

The young woman swooned to think of herself so full of strength and power. She imagined herself stepping into a room and all heads turning to notice her. Her nostrils flaring, she would shake her hair; she would move across the room with all eyes watching her.

Then she looked down. A new button had appeared on the Universal Remote. It read "Past" and blinked at her with an urgent red light. The woman pressed the button, and the image of the stallion danced before her as if it were one of her very own holographic movies.

The stallion was a Byerly Turk thoroughbred, sixteen

hundred pounds of grace and power. He had a white blaze down his face, three white feet, and a star on the heel of the leg that was solid black. The horse was a jumper, and he cleared walls, fences, and water troughs with ease.

Holding the "Past" button down, the woman could see the day the man had decided to buy the horse.

"Strong hind quarters," the man had said as he circled around the horse, pushing and slapping each section. "Firm hips and thighs, maybe a touch bandy-legged." The horse brought his hooves together as if to hide the line of his legs. "Good sloping shoulders. Short back. Chest not too narrow."

"Yes," said the man who was selling the horse. "His bones are hard. His croup is high. His body deep."

The horse lowered his face as if embarrassed by their comments.

Next, the woman saw the lengthy days of practice. The man led the horse on a long line and cracked a whip on the ground to encourage the horse to keep moving over larger and larger obstacles. In one scene the man came to get the horse out of a pasture, but the horse did not want to go. "Champions don't hesitate," the man had whispered into the young horse's ear. The man told the horse stories of other thoroughbreds who had injured tendons or even broken legs but still fought on to win the race.

In the next scene the horse paced across a show ring, and hundreds of people clapped and chattered about the horse's "beautiful lines." In the competition to see how quickly the horse could obey his master's commands, the horse was judged on how high and how fast he could jump, as well as how accurately he could perform circles and figure-eights. At that competition the horse had won two blue ribbons, and with that his resale value had doubled as well.

Then the image of the horse dissolved in front of the woman, melting into the haze of the rising morning sun.

"This heart could be yours," the man was still saying and held the heart eye level to the woman. It beat with such power that the woman could only stare at the huge heart.

The man continued speaking, "Of course, you'll travel with me wherever I go so that everyone can see my beautiful companion."

"What?" the woman asked as if finally waking. "What are you saying?"

The man moved toward her, holding the stallion's heart in his hand. "Don't worry. We can make it fit." As he moved closer, the woman sensed the beat of that heart pulsing into her own body. "And the fame," the man said. "You won't believe the attention and the awards you'll receive."

The heart was moving closer and closer to her chest.

"I'm the best trainer in town," the man was saying and moved ever closer, holding out the stallion's heart. "A tough task-master but I get results. I get the job done."

The man was only inches from her face. It was as if the woman could feel the horse's heart inside her, a sharp, knife-like pain between her breasts. Quickly the woman punched the "Danger" button on the Universal Remote.

The man completely disappeared. He left no trace except one small drop of blood on the woman's pillow, a drop that had fallen from the thoroughbred's heart.

❖

During that day the woman sat quietly, hardly moving from the spot where she had lain the night before. She was not even aware of any thoughts in her head. She spent lots of time staring and taking naps and floating in the stream. She could see that her oasis was only temporary and that soon the hot desert sun would dry up the river, but for the moment she could not even find the energy to worry.

Then that night, just as she was drifting off to sleep, the woman was once again awakened by footsteps—footsteps that moved slowly as if the feet were being dragged across the sand. *Scru-unch-squeak. Scru-unch-squeak. Scru-unch-squeak.*

Walking toward her was an old woman dressed in a robe of heron-grey blue. The old woman's body rose up from the sand, then curved back to the ground, her head lower then her shoulders, as though she had buckled from the weight of the robe. In one hand the old woman held a walking stick. In the other she carried a heart. Beating gently, the heart glowed in the dark with a brilliant light.

"I won't be needing this heart now," the old woman said. "And it could be yours. It seems a shame to put so much intelligence into it and then just let it wither when I die. And with a heart like this, you'll have already learned everything you need to know. You'll never again have to struggle with why things are the way they are. People will listen to you. They'll come from all around to get help with their problems."

The woman swooned to think of herself so intelligent and so sure of herself. She imagined herself at a meeting of world leaders, all wanting her advice, all hanging on her every word. The Universal Remote flashed, and the woman pressed the button marked "Past."

THE WOMAN WHO LOST HER HEART

It was just as the old woman said—she *was* incredibly smart. At a younger age, the old woman had taught at the finest universities. She had worked on the design for the tower cities that were to float in Lake Michigan. She had solved the gravitational pull problem for a proposed space station's docking ports. Still pressing the button marked "Past," the woman could see the old woman standing before a blackboard filled with equations. Hundreds of experts shouted questions at her. She wrote more equations. The experts sighed with satisfaction.

But it was not just in work situations that the old woman had excelled. In the next scene the old woman was helping her niece plan her wedding. "I'll just add a few touches," the old woman was telling her niece. "Just a few things that will make people talk about your wedding for the rest of their lives." They both laughed, and the old woman was back at the blackboard, this time planning her niece's wedding with flow charts that looked as complex as inter-planetary travel maps. The old woman had decided on a progressive dinner party for her niece's reception. Using the newly-opened TUBE that transported people underground from Chicago to New York in just nine hours, the old woman had planned for the three hundred guests to eat a different dinner course in each major city along the way. Her niece was astounded!

"This heart could be yours," the old woman was saying as the scenes from the past disappeared. "Why, it's nothing to put a new heart in these days. Of course, you'll need some kind of raised platform to sit on. And some kind of sign-up system because people will want to speak with you privately.

And a very tough security system. I can recommend a good agency."

"What?" the woman asked, and she heard her voice crack. "What are you saying?"

The old woman moved closer, holding the glowing heart out. "Oh, absolutely," she said, "a good scheduler and a good security guard. Those are the two most important things." The old woman stretched the heart out to the woman. "Don't worry now, this won't take up much room."

The heart moved closer and closer, and the woman began to back away. "Smart girl like you," the old woman wheedled, "think of all the things you'll know, all the things you'll be able to do." It was as though the woman could feel the beat of the old woman's heart pulsing in her own chest, the beat of an icy, cold heart. The woman grabbed for the

Universal Remote. It wasn't there! She had dropped it!

The old woman's heart was only inches from the woman's chest. The woman leaned to the side and dove for the remote. Rolling over onto her back, the woman could see the old woman flying through the air, lunging at her with the heart extended, descending toward her, speeding toward her, about to pierce her chest. The woman punched the Universal Remote. "Danger! Danger!" she cried as she pushed at the button.

When the woman opened her eyes, the old woman had completely disappeared. She left no trace except a breath of cold air rising like mist in the early morning sun.

All that day the woman sat and cried. She did not even know why she was crying, and usually she could not tolerate not knowing why. But she felt so weak she gave up trying to figure out what was going on.

"That's two," the woman said out loud. "One more heart will come my way. And if that one isn't right, what do I do then?"

The woman let her tears fall, and that night instead of resting her head on her pillow, the woman lay on her side, drew up her legs, and cradled the pillow into her middle. She slept all night with her arms wrapped around it. The woman slept soundly until she heard footsteps once again.

CHAPTER FOUR

ctually, the woman heard giggles and singing before she heard footsteps.

"La-la-la-li-li . . ."

It was the sound of a child's voice, light and happy-sounding, floating out into the quiet desert on the first glow of daylight. Off in the distance, coming over the low rise of a sand dune, the woman could barely make out the figure of a little girl coming toward her, a little girl who could not have been more than three years old.

"La-la-la-li-li," the child sang, sometimes skipping and even turning as she danced down the sand dune toward the woman.

"La-la-la-li-li . . ."

As the girl came closer, the woman felt a tremor run through her body. Could it be? She sat up and leaned forward, staring into the faint beginnings of daylight, straining to see the face of the child coming toward her. As the little girl stepped out of the shadows, the woman's breath rushed out in astonishment.

The child was herself, dressed as she had been for her first formal photograph. She was wearing the antique white dress her grandmother had left her. It was gauzy white cotton with puffy sleeves, and lace trimming the edges of the collar. When she came close enough to see the woman, the child stopped and smiled.

"You're looking for your heart, aren't 'cha?" the little girl asked and held out a flat clay heart painted a deep cherry-red. Pressed into the heart was a small handprint. The child set the object down in the sand and, squatting next to it, carefully placed her palm into the handprint.

"There!" she laughed and looked up into the woman's face, beaming. "See. My hand fits. I made it. I made it for you."

The woman felt her body tighten as she stood up to approach the little girl and the heart of clay. Then she touched her own chest and once again felt the emptiness where her heart used to be.

"I don't understand," the woman said as panic seized her body. "Is this it? Is this the third heart? It's not real."

"I made it for you," the child repeated and looked up at the woman.

"But what good is it going to do me?" the woman shrieked. "I can't live with that. It's not beating. It's not alive. Is this my last choice? Did you waste my last choice with a . . . a hunk of clay?"

The child recoiled as though she had been slapped. She hid her head in her arms, crouching in front of the woman who was standing over her.

"Tell me!" The woman was yelling now. "What am I supposed to do with *this*?"

"Nothing," the little girl said, a sob breaking into her voice as she quickly snatched the object off the sand. Holding it tightly in both hands, the little girl stood up and backed away from the woman. By this time, she was crying. "If you don't want it," she managed to say between sobs, "then you don't have to take it!"

The child turned and ran. Up the dune she went. She moved for a time along the ridge, her slight body a small silhouette against the eastern sky. Then she was gone.

❖

The woman sank to her knees in the sand, her body bent over, her chest collapsed. A sob welled up in her throat. "What have I done? I shouldn't have yelled at her like that. How could I?"

"*SIT UP!*"

The voice boomed out of the morning air, clear and incredibly loud. The sound reverberated up the woman's spine, and she found herself bolt upright, tingling from head to toe. Sitting in front of her, looking her straight in the eye, sat a Robed Figure, its head and shoulders covered with a dark shawl. Its face was nearly hidden as it spoke, "You so rarely hear me anymore."

"Hear you?" the woman managed to sputter out. "I don't even know you."

"You speak more truth than you know. I was trying to talk to you through the Universal Remote. When the 'Fear' button was blinking, that was me. When you ignore what you feel, you lose one of the main ways I can guide you."

"I'm sorry, but the only kind of guidance I need right now is how to find a heart."

"All right," the Robed Figure said sadly and began to fade away, "though a heart is one of the easier things to find."

"Wait!" the woman yelled and reached out to touch

the Figure's shawl. "Don't go. Maybe you *can* help me."

Like a holographic fade-in, the Figure slowly returned until it sat again in front of her, a smile on its face.

"I never go away," the Figure said. "I am always with you, inside of you. I just hoped that if I appeared on the outside, I might get your attention."

"You have my attention," the woman sighed tiredly. "What was that you said?"

"When you would not admit you were afraid, the sand piled up and buried the remote. When you pressed the 'Fear' button, it brought the rain."

"No. Not about the remote. What did you say about it being easy to find a heart?"

"Finding a heart is easy. Keeping the life running through it as one grows older, that is the trick."

"What's the trick?" the woman asked exasperated.

"Your mentor already told you."

"What? She told me to be aware and breathe, um, feel and heal, uh, and open and grow. But what does that have to do with anything? How can I do all that without a heart?"

"No, it is the other way around. You will never find your heart until you follow those steps. Start with step one. If you are truly aware of where you are and where you have been, you will discover the way to the child again."

"You mean that clay heart *was* my last choice? That was it?" The woman stood up and brushed the sand from her clothes. "But the child's run off. How can I find her?"

"Start with where you are."

"I'm in a desert!"

"What do you see?"

"I see the desert!"

"No. You do not see what is here," the Robed One said and, from the sleeve of its robe, the Figure produced a small bird. "Follow the desert woodpecker, this gilded flicker. He will show you what the desert is all about."

"I don't need a tour guide. I need a heart!"

But the Robed Figure ignored the woman, dissolved into the quiet desert air, and disappeared as quickly as it had come.

"Oh, great," the woman said and looked up to see the gilded flicker circling overhead. The woman stubbornly crossed her arms. "I don't want to go anywhere else," she called to it. "Go ahead. You leave, too."

As if taking her at her word, the bird began to fly away.

"No, wait! I'm coming. I'm coming," the woman

sighed. Following a woodpecker about the desert seemed useless to the woman but, suddenly, being left alone seemed an even worse prospect.

"Do you talk, too?" she called to the bird, but it only turned back to look at her, then fluttered ahead. "All right. I don't care who or what you are. Just bring me to the heart."

The woman scooted over the scorching sand, for the gilded flicker was moving quickly. She was not sure what was hotter—the heat from the sun or the heat coming off the ground. After traveling at this pace for a while, the woman and the bird came to a stand of saguaro, some of the cacti fifty feet tall. They were planted evenly, ninety feet or so apart, as if a gardener had intentionally landscaped them that way. Extended from a saguaro's accordion-pleated stem was a waxy green branch, thick and long enough to provide a strip of shade. The woman hopped under it and felt the temperature around her and under her feet drop a few comforting degrees. She looked up and watched the woodpecker dive into a nest in the cactus.

"Okay, we'll rest for a while," the woman thought. She sat down on her haunches and watched other woodpeckers drilling holes into the cacti around her. The sap oozing from the holes formed a leathery scar tissue that made sturdy, resin-like homes for the birds.

"Well, come on, buddy," she called up to the wood-pecker. "Let's get on with it. I don't know how much time I have left to find this heart."

There was no sound and no movement from the nest above her. The woman wrapped her arms around her knees and stared out from her protective bit of shade.

"What do you see?" she said aloud, mocking the Robed Figure's question. "I see the desert," she answered the Figure who was not there. "I see the stupid desert I'm stuck in."

But as she stared across the stand of saguaro, the woman thought she might be hallucinating. The ground in front of her and next to her seemed to be shifting. She looked closer and realized that a spadefoot toad was burrowing deeper into the cooler sand. Nearby a gopher and a tarantula spider were lying in forced inactivity. The ground was filled with living things that dared not move.

Then she remembered the narrator in the holographic film series she produced on "The Great Deserts of the World" saying, "During the dry times, plants cannot afford ornaments of leaves and flowers. Pretty green leaves and colorful flowers allow too much water to evaporate. The living things of the desert program themselves to need less. The finest example is the kangaroo rat, a mouse that has taught itself to live without water. With camouflage, the lizards and rock-squirrels evade the desert stalkers but surrender their individuality. With their daily burrowing in, the gophers, the spiders, and the spadefoot toad survive but surrender their right to thrive. Relentlessly, the sun speaks out the logic of the desert: hoard, hold back, hide."

The gilded flicker appeared and chirped loudly at the woman, almost squawking. It hopped from root to root of a fallen saguaro and, suddenly, the woman understood why the cacti were spaced as they were. She began to pull at the roots of the saguaro that were still in the ground. They were easy to yank out of the sand—the roots spread horizontally only seven or so inches deep into the ground.

"Such shallow roots for such a tall cactus," the woman said aloud. The web of roots extended about forty-five feet in all directions to where it met the next cactus's root system. Nothing could grow in between. Each saguaro had marked out its turf, defended its ground, won the solitary struggle to fight for and protect its water rights by keeping its neighbors away. Each saguaro with its labyrinth of roots stood poised to hoard whatever trinket of nourishment might come its way.

"Each cactus for itself," the woman said and put her face into the crook of her arm. The sand blew past her and began to swirl as the woman made out the faint voice of the Robed Figure once again.

"Does this remind you of home?" the Robed Figure asked.

"What? There's no drought at home," the woman

snapped.

"If we do not pay attention to the signs, things tend to get worse," the Figure said. A shower of sand swept in front of the Robed Figure. The floor of the desert seemed to rise in sheets in front of the woman.

"Where are you?" the woman shouted as the Robed Figure disappeared in a crosscurrent of grainy whirlwinds.

"Where are *you*?" the Robed One called back.

"Apparently I'm in the middle of a sandstorm," the woman cried, fell to her knees, and covered her head. Her mouth and the inside of her nostrils were caked with sand. "I don't know what you want."

"I want your breath; I want your awareness."

"I can't talk. I can't even think," the woman gasped. "This sand is driving me out of my mind."

"That is a start," the Robed Figure said.

The woman felt the last drops of moisture leave her mouth. Then the sand in front of the woman lifted and took on the shape of a whirling spout. "Can you stop it?" the woman called to the Robed Figure. "We'll be buried alive."

The funnel of twisting sand lifted into the air, then changed direction downward, drilling a huge crater into the ground. With a sound like hundreds of locomotives groaning through the night, the tornado of sand plunged into the earth, pulling one saguaro after another into its cavity.

"Follow," the Robed Figure said. The woman looked up and saw the Robed One, full and present, standing in front of her.

"In there?" the woman asked and pointed into the imploding pit. "Are you crazy?"

"Deeper into the desert," the Robed Figure said. "It is how you get out of the storm."

"No way," the woman said, ducked her face into her knees, and pulled her arms tighter about her head.

"When your eyes are truly opened," the Robed One continued as though the woman had not spoken, "you will understand why you refused the horse trainer's and the old woman's hearts."

Before the woman could respond, the ground beneath her gave way, as if the earth wanted to reclaim her, sucking her further into its depths.

CHAPTER FIVE

t first it was like sliding in the dark down a chute of sand. But then the woman straddled thin air with nothing below her body. She fell end over end until she thought she would pass out from fright and dizziness.

"Trust that something will catch you," she heard the Robed Figure saying. She could not tell where the Robed One was, only that its voice surrounded her.

"Ri-i-ight!" the woman screamed, still falling, her

voice echoing through the tunnel. She could not make this free fall come out right. Nothing to push off of, nothing to grab onto, nothing to tell if there would be an end to this tumbling at all. She willed herself to spread her arms and legs out full to stop her somersaulting, to steady herself like a skydiver hovering above a moonless earth. As she opened her body a bit and leaned into the fall, fingers of light shot up from below her, rays of brilliance intertwined into a soft, glowing mattress of light. She fell through layer after layer of radiance, the glow breaking her fall until she landed on her side as gently as an infant being laid down for a nap. The woman opened her eyes and found herself lying on the very bed she had slept in as a child.

"See how quickly the kids develop when they work out in those ultra-gravity rooms," she heard her father saying in the next room. "Look at those calves, huh?"

The woman got up from the bed and walked into the living room. There she saw her father, her mother, several family friends, and herself as a child about nine years old.

"They don't see you," the Robed Figure whispered as it appeared at the woman's side.

"They look so young," was all the woman could say. "My parents. They look so young."

"She's lifting two hundred pounds," her mother bragged. "Just look at those shoulders."

One family friend, a man with a short curly beard, stepped toward the little girl, and her parents nodded to their daughter to flex her muscles so he could feel them.

"Oh no!" the woman shrieked. "I never liked him! I hated him touching me!" And then the woman noticed the look on the little girl's face. The little girl flexed her arms, made her muscles as tight as rocks. She smiled and laughed along with her parents, but as the man squeezed her body, the little girl's lips were pursed and her eyes squinted closed.

"She is no longer there," the Robed Figure explained.

Though the little girl's body had frozen, her mind had not. The woman could hear the little girl's thoughts: "Mommy and Daddy love me when I do well. I have to prove that I'm okay."

"She's going to take State," her mother was saying.

"Are you kidding? She's going to take the Nationals," her father boasted. "That's what she's training for now. Right, honey? Keep your eye on the big prize. Never settle for less. Practice, practice, practice."

The man with the beard continued to push at the little

girl's biceps and calves, and as he did, another scene came up behind the one in the living room. In the background the woman could see the horse trainer and his stallion. The trainer walked around the horse pushing at each muscle group and slapping the horse on the rear. Then he swung onto the horse's back, yanked the horse's bit roughly, and dug his metal stirrups into the horse's side. It was the time of year when the other thoroughbreds were given a rest period to run free without shoes, allowed to race unshod in the lush, green pastures. The horse trainer refused to give the stallion such a rest. "His left flank needs tightening," the trainer explained to his assistant. "We have to work on his gait. He'll never capture the title if we don't change his rhythm."

"Her waist could use a little tightening," the man with the beard was saying. He poked a finger into the little girl's stomach, and everyone in the living room laughed.

"I had to look just right," the woman sobbed in a flash of understanding. "People examined my body as if I were an animal."

"You had to perform," the Robed Figure added. "Maybe that is why the horse's heart frightened you so."

"And the other heart?" the woman asked, changing the subject. She searched for the "Off" button on the Universal Remote, and when she pressed it, the images from the past disappeared. "What was so bad about the old woman's heart?"

"First of all," the Figure said, "she is not so old. She is only a bit older than you."

"But she looked ancient, and she said she was going to die."

"Yes," the Robed Figure agreed, "she is not going to

last much longer. Very little juice runs through that old woman's heart." The Robed Figure took the remote out of the woman's hand, pressed the "On" button, and another scene from the woman's childhood appeared.

The little girl was playing by a river, building a dam of sticks, mud, and sand. The image evolved over hours of play, and the muddy dam turned into an entire city with twig bridges and leafy, shaded canopies. Then the little girl's parents appeared in the scene.

"What do you think you're doing going off like that on your own and wasting the day? Playing in the mud!" they exclaimed. "Is that going to get you anything? You're supposed to be working on the Boards."

The little girl had been told repeatedly that most children began studying for the College Board entrance exams when they were six years old. She followed her parents back to their house and sat in front of the computer for the rest of the day. The woman could hear the little girl's thoughts: "I have to know everything. When I do what feels good to me, Mommy and Daddy get mad."

Her father walked into the room and put his hand on his daughter's shoulder. "We're depending on you," he said.

"I'll figure it out, Dad," the little girl said and doubled her efforts to get everything done. Other images began to play in the background, pictures from the old woman's life. The old woman stood in front of a blackboard, presenting her latest findings to her academic colleagues. In a flurry of wild chalk marks, the old woman filled the board with mathematical formulas and diagrams. The woman could hear the old woman thinking, "I have to know everything," and watched the old

woman panic when she didn't know an answer to her colleagues' questions, even lying at times to cover her ignorance.

People such as the niece did come to the old woman
for advice, but actually they resented the old woman's efforts
to take over, to move them and their lives about like so many
chess pieces.

"Just like my younger sisters resented me," the
woman mused. "They said I was always trying to run their
lives. But if I hadn't done it, who would? Nothing would have
gotten done."

"But some part of you was frightened by the old
woman's heart. Some part of you knew it was just more of the
same," the Robed Figure reminded her.

"Maybe. But what good does it do to see these things
now?" the woman asked. "These images are like my holo-

graphic films; they aren't real."

"Not real?" the Robed Figure asked.

"You know," the woman said, "not happening now."

The Robed Figure pushed another button on the Universal Remote, and images swirled around them, 3-D and 360 degrees: the little girl destroying her mud city; the little girl spending hours in the ultra-gravity practice rooms; the little girl studying late into the night at her computer; the little girl being grilled on what she had accomplished that day; the little girl standing at attention before her parents, paralyzed by their messages that now twisted around the woman in giant, 3-D letters and blasted in ear-splitting stereophonic sound, "Do more. Be more. Make us be proud of you."

The woman swatted her hands through the images, but her hands slid through the 3-D pictures like water. "Turn it off! Turn it off!" the woman screamed. "These things are in the past! Let them stay in the past!"

"Are they?" the Robed Figure shouted and pressed the remote button marked "Present."

Weaving through and around the images from her childhood were scenes from the woman's life just two weeks earlier. The woman watched herself straining to concentrate as she edited holographic films into the early morning hours, her fifth straight all-nighter to meet a contest deadline. During her "breaks," the woman saw herself standing in front of the goal chart on her wall, moving the magnetic stick-ons around, scheduling her life.

The woman could hear her own thoughts roaring as she edited the film. "We'll never make the entry date. If I don't get this done, what will they think of me? We *have* to take first place like we did last year. Maybe we should have entered three films instead of just two."

Then superimposed over the woman's face came the faces of the horse trainer, the old woman, her mother and her father. Simultaneously, their mouths and her mouth screamed the words, "Perform! Keep it together! Figure it out!"

The woman whirled around in the middle of all the images, trying to find the Robed Figure. "But I've got to make an extra effort to get these big projects done," the woman shouted over the din. "What's the use of doing something, if it's not the best? I've *got* to keep track of everything. If I don't do it, who will? That's my job!"

The images swirled back through time. The woman could see each generation in her family turn to the next generation, hissing the words, "Do it yourself. Understand everything. Make us look good." And then she could see all the people with whom her ancestors had come in contact—teachers, bosses, parents, friends—mouthing the words, "Produce. Succeed. It's all up to you." From her great-great-grandparents to her great-grandparents to her grandparents to her parents, until finally, centuries of words piled on top of the little girl. And the child repeated the phrases by rote and grew into the adult woman who only moments before had said, "If I don't do it, who will?" and "What's the use of doing something, if it's not the best?" Everywhere she turned, the woman saw images of herself through infancy, early adulthood, and then, all around her, instant replays of herself only seconds before.

"Stop!" she finally screamed, so disoriented in time that she fell to her knees. "Stop! Enough! I get the picture!"

"Do you?" she heard the Robed Figure ask, and suddenly they were alone, encased in silence.

"Do you?" the Robed Figure repeated. "Do you understand?"

"Well, just give me a moment here to think," the woman said, and she sat down on what was now the desert floor. "I'll figure it out."

"Then you do not need me," the Robed Figure sighed and began slowly fading away.

"Wait!" the woman cried. "What about the heart? How am I going to find the child who has my heart? You said it was easy to find a heart, but I'm right back where I started." The woman looked up and saw the bare octotillo bush in front of her.

"Walk," the Robed Figure said faintly, barely an outline now.

"Walk?" the woman shouted at the fading image. "That's all I've been doing."

"Walk," the Robed Figure repeated, "until you find a new way of traveling."

And then the Robed Figure was gone.

CHAPTER SIX

t was a long walk. The heat from the ground burned through the woman's thin shoes, but the Universal Remote came once again to her rescue. One red light blinked softly "Boots" and another blinked "Stick." A pair of high-tech hiking boots appeared, the kind that carried a computer chip for continuous adjustment of the inner padding to the wearer's foot. Along with the boots came a sturdy walking stick. It was almost as long as the woman was tall and just the right thickness for her hand to grasp comfortably.

She decided to travel with the sun at her back, so it would not beat so unmercifully on her face. But as the day wore on, the woman realized there was no way to escape the heat. The desert stretched out on every side, the same parched land everywhere, except for an outcropping of red rock rising ahead of her. If she could just climb that, surely on the other side she would find shade.

It was not until she used the walking stick to pull herself up the rock ledges that the woman noticed the face of a snake carved into it. The long shape of the snake's head followed the curves and grooves in the end of the stick, and its eyes seemed to look deep inside her when she turned the stick just so.

"This must be what I'm supposed to be doing," she

told herself as she climbed the rocky ridge. "The remote gave me these incredible boots and this great walking stick." She stopped to catch her breath, but her mind raced on. "I don't really know what I'm doing. I don't know where I am. I don't know where I'm going."

The woman tried to calm herself. "Okay. Take one thing at a time. Find some shade. Just make it to the other side of the ridge." She felt in her pocket to see if the remote was still there. "Then see what's blinking on the remote. Water, I hope. And food." Her mentor's face flashed in front of her eyes.

"Do you have any idea what I'm going through?" she asked out loud. "Do you know what it's like out here? At least three nights in the Great Valley, you said. Well, I've been here a lifetime and more."

The woman turned to look behind her at the sun. But now it was blazing down from directly overhead. Her own body scarcely made a shadow. "Great! I've walked all morning to find some shade, and now it's noon. There's no shade any-where." With one final thrust of her walking stick, the woman struggled onto the top of the ridge. "And here I am, stuck on this rockpile in the middle of . . ."

She stopped in mid-sentence and stared at the scene below her. She was looking down into a canyon of red rock. Flowing through the canyon was a narrow river, its current moving fast enough to break occasionally over large stones in its path. Lying on one of the banks, its green hull standing out against the reddish sand, was a canoe.

"Aha, a different way of traveling!" the woman said. She saw brightly colored supply bags piled next to the canoe and knew she would find the food and equipment she needed. "Let's just hope this is the last leg of the journey." She began climbing down to the river bank, calmer now and filled with new energy. As she placed the walking stick on the rocks below her for support, she saw the snake's eyes glinting at her in the noonday sun.

After drinking her fill from the river, it didn't take the woman long to load the supplies into the middle of the canoe. The paddle was just her size. It brought back memories of canoeing at summer camp when she was a child. But the camp had been for budding gymnasts such as herself, and so the woman had not spent much time on the water. "It'll all come back to me," she said to herself as she tucked her walking stick up under her arm and pushed the canoe out from shore.

The current caught the canoe suddenly and began to

propel it downstream. "This water is faster than it looks," the woman thought. "I don't even have to paddle." She felt the water pull her along.

"Put on your life jacket," something told her. "Never go in a boat without one." She had thrown the life jacket into the bottom of the canoe, and now as she was swept along, she reached for it and put it on.

Since the canyon was so deep and narrow, the sun could not find the water for whole stretches of river. The woman felt bathed in cool air. The motion of the canoe created a little breeze, and she lay back against the end of the canoe and sighed. She was about to close her eyes when she noticed a sound—low, rumbling, and distant. And then the canoe swerved suddenly, and she heard a long scrape against its bottom.

"Shallow. It's shallow here. Maybe I should practice some strokes." The woman sat up and reached for the paddle. The distant sound seemed louder to her now, but she was concentrating more on trying to guide the canoe. It wasn't easy. The current was swift. The canoe constantly bumped and scraped, and when she tried pushing the paddle away from her or pulling it in toward the canoe, she often struck bottom.

Ahead of her now she could see the tips of rocks just breaking the surface of the water. When she tried to miss them, it didn't work. The current pulled her just in the direction she did not want to go. In spite of her stroking with the paddle, the river pulled and scraped the canoe over rocks she could see, and over others she did not even know were there.

And the sound. The sound had definitely grown louder. It seemed to echo off the steep walls of the canyon ahead of her, a long insistent booming in her ears. She realized that the turn in the river that had seemed so far in the distance was just ahead. As she rounded the curve, the current swept her out toward the far bank and began to turn the canoe sideways.

Ahead of her now was nothing but surging white water and foaming rapids. The water broke over the sides of the canoe, spraying into her face as she shot through the narrowest part of the canyon. The canoe whirled, turning from side to back to front again, pitching and rolling over rocks that cracked against its sides. Then the riverbed dropped sharply, and the force of the current plunging downhill sent water shooting up the sides of the canyon walls. Torrents of water fell back into the river like a huge downpour, drenching the woman and battering the canoe.

The sound was deafening. It boomed and pounded around her, rocketing back and forth off the canyon walls. In the midst of this swirling frenzy, the woman looked down to see her hands gripping the gunnels of the canoe.

"My paddle! My paddle! I don't have my paddle!"

The woman screamed. She rode the canoe like a carnival tilt-a-whirl, her head thrown back, her mouth opened wide. She screamed until there was no more breath in her. When air rushed back into her lungs, she screamed again. The canoe hit full force against a large boulder, and its side was dented by the strength of the blow. The woman was thrown forward into the middle of the canoe, and as she reached for the sides, a voice pounded into her ear.

"Keep the bow pointed downstream! You're doing it wrong!"

Rising out of the river, a swell of water hung over the woman. It grew larger, taking on the appearance of a long, thick neck. Out of the surging water at the end of the neck, a face grew, contorted and huge, yelling at the woman, "Paddle faster! Do what I tell you! You're doing it wrong!"

"Help me!" the woman yelled back. "I don't have a paddle!" The pounding water drenched her, and the huge face faded into the spray. With a wrench the canoe swung loose from the boulder and headed downstream, backward. The woman lay in the canoe, sprawled on her back, and a new watery, transparent face loomed over her.

"Hold on to your paddle!" it shrieked. "What's wrong with you? You know better. Hold on to your paddle!"

"What paddle? *It's gone! It's lost!* I don't *have* a paddle!"

Another downpour of water from the canyon wall

struck the canoe and sent it spinning. Both faces now appeared over her, distorted grimaces spreading out in the spray and calling to her in a jumble of pounding water, "You can do better than that. I thought you knew how to do this. You're doing it all wrong."

"You - aren't - helping - me!"

The woman's body bowed upward in the canoe. Her hands on the gunnels, her feet planted on the bottom, she lifted herself off the floor, pushed her chest into the air, and from every inch of her body there came a bellow of rage.

"Look - at - me! I - need - help! I don't care what you think I *should* do!" And with each slap of the canoe against a rock, with each drenching of water in her face, the woman yelled back. She yelled with all her force into the surging current and the pounding spray. "Stop this! Stop it!

Just stop!"

With a slam the canoe catapulted out over a ledge in the river and hung there a moment, its bow tipping toward the water below. The woman screamed again as the canoe flew out into the air, one last surge of current sending it over the edge.

When she hit the water, the woman realized that she had been thrown completely clear of the canoe. Wherever it had landed, she was nowhere near it. She lay on her back in a deep pool of quiet backwater. All she could see were the vertical walls of the canyon rising above her and far above the walls, a strip of pale blue sky.

The roar of white water was receding now. Her life jacket was keeping her afloat. The woman could barely move. She was completely exhausted, drained. "Not one thing more," she thought. "Not one thing more can happen to me because I can't fight back anymore. I just can't." And she let her arms spread out in the quiet pool and her head tilt back until the water covered her ears. She felt totally helpless floating there with no strength to resist the helplessness. A sound welled up in her, and she heard a tiny cry escape from her lips. So soft that sound, like the cry of an infant. Although stiff and aching, her body felt small and young.

"This is how I felt as a baby," she thought. "This is how I was as a child." And a small cry came again from her lips. But this time the tears came, too. Not great sobs, for she had no strength to cry like that. Instead, the tears rolled slowly down the sides of her face and into the water covering her ears. And she let herself feel, for the first time, the empty space where her heart had been. She let herself feel the loneliness that had been there all her life.

With no strength to push the loneliness away, no energy left to bury it, she could at last feel grief. She felt the ache of it move out of the muscles of her throat, where she had held back for so long, and into her entire body. She felt her awareness leap across nerve endings to places it had never been before. And she found sadness hidden in her back, her belly, her thighs. It began to seep out of her bones until her whole body vibrated with feeling. There was no holding it back. And then slowly the connections came.

"I was so lonely when I was little. I didn't even know how lonely I was. I needed a lot of help, but I didn't know how to ask. I needed a lot of love, but I didn't know where it was."

The woman felt her throat tighten again as the memories began to spill over each other.

"Feel. Just feel," a voice inside her said. And the memories faded as the woman turned her awareness once more to her body, which was now flowing with grief.

CHAPTER SEVEN

 he woman felt barely conscious of her physical surroundings, so deeply had she been focusing on her body.

"Move. You have to move *now*," the voice inside her said. "You know that a slow chill in an exhausted body can kill. Get out of the cold water. Do it now."

The woman heard a crackling sound behind her. As she rolled over in the water, she saw a campfire burning on the shore at the edge of the pool. Beside the fire, neatly stacked, sat the supply bags she had loaded into the canoe.

It was all the woman could do to swim to the edge of the pool and pull herself out of the water. In the supply bags she found clothes and food. When she changed into the dry clothes, she saw the bruises on her body from the canoe ride, but nothing more.

As she moved slowly to prepare a meal, she knew her body had changed. Something had been wrestled out of her, shaken out of her very being. And there was room now for something new. As she knelt by the fire to feed more wood into the flames, she felt gratitude warm the place where her heart had been.

"I don't know who or what has been doing this, but something has been protecting me all along," she realized.

"You are right," the voice inside her said. The woman

recognized the Robed Figure's voice. She looked around her to make sure the familiar figure was not sitting somewhere on a rock close by. Then the woman smiled. "You really are inside, and I can hear you now."

"Dry out your boots. We are not finished yet," the inner voice advised. "I know it seems like forever, but when I first appeared, you were looking for . . . "

". . . for her! For the little girl." The woman felt an ache in the middle of her chest. "I feel so badly," the woman said. "I've got to find her. I don't care about the clay heart. I just want to tell her that I'm sorry for how I've treated her."

The woman filled a backpack with what she thought she'd need. She found her walking stick tucked carefully among the supplies. She put out the fire and, as she was about to leave, remembered to pull the Universal Remote out of the pocket of the wet trousers she was leaving behind. Holding the walking stick firmly in her hand, she asked herself which way to go.

It was the stick that answered. It turned ever so slightly in her hand so that the eyes of the snake looked toward a narrow ledge on the canyon wall. She knew then which way to climb, and when she reached that ledge, the stick showed her the way to the top of the canyon.

When she reached the summit, the woman looked out into another time and place. It was a land of country gardens and old stone walls separating rolling fields of green. On a lane that ran beside one of the old walls, the woman saw a small figure.

"La-la-la-li-li. La-la-la-li-li."

The child was skipping as she sang, skipping away

from the woman who called out to her.

"Wait! Don't go!"

The child stopped, turned, and looked at the woman from a distance. Then the child whirled and ran. The woman threw off her backpack, and using her walking stick, she started after the child as fast as she could go. Once on the lane, she began to run. The child ran faster. With one last look into the eyes of the snake, the woman threw the walking stick into a grove of low bushes and raced after the girl.

❖

The child left the lane, and the woman had to follow her through thick underbrush and prickly brambles. She hardly felt the thorns scratching her arms and legs. Up ahead she could still see the little girl.

"Wait!" she called, but the child kept running.

Finally the woman felt as though she could run no longer. She stopped to catch her breath in a garden choked with weeds and overgrown bushes. The child was gone, nowhere in sight. The garden was still. "Where are you?" the woman gasped. "I . . . I . . . I love you. Don't run away. Please don't run away!"

Then the woman spotted the lace of the child's frilly dress behind a crumbling stone wall. The woman raced to the child and saw her crouched against the wall, arms crossed, her face still furious.

"All right. All right," said the woman, "we'll take it slow. I'll just be here on the other side of the wall. You don't have to come out until you're ready."

"Who says I'm ever going to be ready?" the child

shouted.

"Whoa! You *are* angry," the woman said. "That's okay. We can both be angry and we'll work things out."

"Sure," the child responded.

"Look," said the woman as she settled down on the other side of the wall, "I'm sorry I didn't want your heart. I was scared and I said things I shouldn't have. And I know it's not just this one time. I know I've said mean things and left you alone too often. But I'm here to take care of you now. I want to do things differently."

"Words are easy," the little girl said in a whisper.

"Well then, how can I show you?" The woman waited for an answer, but none came back to her. Instead, there was a rustling sound. The woman thought perhaps the child was deciding to come out from behind the wall, but the sound was too dense, too heavy for such a little girl. A sense of danger pierced the woman's being. She jumped up, peered over the wall, and saw the back of a huge, leathery green dragon, its large head wrenching from side to side, breathing fire into the air. She could not see the little girl.

Before the woman could say anything or even make a move, the dragon was gone, stalking off through the weedy garden. The woman stood there frozen with fear and disbelief.

"No-oo-oo-oo!" she finally screamed and, thinking only of the child, rushed after the dragon. "Bring her back!"

The woman could see the dragon lumbering ahead, making its way across a wide open field, covering great distances with every stride. Each time the woman caught up to where she thought the dragon should be, she saw nothing. The air around her hung crisp and still, no breeze to carry a smell or a sound. Then she spotted an opening in the hill, ran to it, and dove in. She shimmied through the tunnel on her belly, her elbows pulling her along. The passageway turned downward, and she was almost sliding, sledding her way into darkness.

The ground beneath her turned to mud. She could hear the dripping sound of running water. Then a shaft of light from somewhere up above allowed her to see ahead into a cave with a cathedral-like ceiling. In the middle of the grand earthen room was a pond where the moisture from the walls of the cave dripped in steady, echoing rhythms. Next to the pond sat the dragon, its back to the woman.

"Give me the child!" the woman yelled, scrambling to her feet. To her left, a glint of something caught the woman's eye. It was a sword, and the woman grabbed for it. The sword was rusty, mangled on the edges, but the woman hoisted it above her head and charged at the dragon. Just as the woman was about to plunge the sword into its back, the dragon craned its large, thick neck backward and breathed a ball of fire that singed the woman's hair and clothes and heated the sword so that the woman had to drop it. The woman continued running without the sword, ramming her body into the dragon's leathery hide. The dragon grabbed for the woman with its webbed paws, and together they tumbled across the floor of the cave and into the pond.

The water was murky, and the woman could see little. With wild, imprecise punches, she wrestled underwater with the dragon. Had the child been pulled into the water with them? Was she still on land? Had she already been eaten? The woman struggled to the surface, desperate for air. She gulped and turned to dive back into the deep water.

When she looked down, it was not the dragon's throat she held between her hands but the fin of a seahag whose tail swished from side to side, whopping against the woman's body as it struggled with all its might. Whatever it was or had become, the woman took the creature down into the water and tightened her hold around its body. She held the hagfish there writhing and turning in her hands until she thought she would run out of breath before it did. Then her hands were pushed apart by the expansion of the seahag's being, and she lost her hold. It was gone. Whatever had been between her hands was gone and rushing to the surface of the water.

The woman followed the motion upward. When she broke through the surface, she saw a giant bat hanging by its claws at the top of the cave, its massive wings wrapped around its body, its head tucked in and invisible. Gasping for air, the woman lifted herself out of the pond and looked around the cave quickly. She could not see the little girl. Was the child wrapped inside the bat's wings or still in the water?

The misshapen sword lay on the ground where she had dropped it. It felt heavier now, and she had to use both hands to lift it. The woman made her way up a steep wall until she was level with the bat. She crawled to the very edge and leaned out, chopping and hacking at the bat's feet.

"Where is she?" she screamed at the creature. "Where is she?"

Finally, the woman knocked the bat loose. It fell head-first to the floor of the cave, a crumbled ball of shiny, black wings, spitting in spasms on the ground. The woman scrambled down to it, lifted the sword over her head, and plunged it at the black sheath in front of her. Just as she did, the sheath peeled back, disintegrated, and there instead of the bat was the little girl. The little girl's torn and bloody face lifted to the woman.

"Will you kill me, too?" the little girl asked.

The woman fell to her knees, dropping the sword beside her, and scooped the child into her arms. "No, no! I wasn't trying to hurt you. I was trying to save you. When I saw the dragon take you . . ."

"I am the dragon," the little girl murmured. Blood streamed from the little girl's mouth. She turned onto her stomach, leaned over the woman's legs, and vomited into the earth. The little girl's entire back was cratered with wounds. "I am the dragon," the child repeated, "the hagfish and the bat. Words are easy," she said and turned her face up to the

133

woman, "but can you love all of me?"

The little girl fainted then, in blessed relief from the pain of her sores and bruises. The woman began to kiss each cut, each bruise, each wound on the child's face and body. She caressed the child's battered flesh with her lips, brushed away dirt with her tongue, held the child to her chest, and rocked her. The child grew limp and heavy in her arms, her breathing shallow and irregular.

"Is it too late?" the woman cried out loud and pulled the child tighter to her breast. "Have I lost you? What can I do?"

The darkness of the cave surrounded her, enveloping her in enough space and enough quiet to sense all, feel all. The voice inside her said, "Go back to the canyon and find the pool." The woman was about to say, "I don't know the way," when she drew in one more breath of nurturing darkness and knew that she would be shown the way.

The woman gently lifted the child's still body onto her back and crawled with her through the cave's narrow passage-way. When they emerged from the cave, she shifted the little girl to the front of her body where she could cradle the child as she walked. She traveled back across the field, through the garden, and up the lane. The woman stopped only to catch her own breath and to try to breathe air into the child. The child appeared dead, but the woman continued to force air into her lungs.

As she breathed, her inner voice told her, "By the way they live, most people fuel their belief in the terror of living. It takes great courage to finish your life larger than when you began. It requires deep trust to take action, to open and grow."

So each time the woman felt panic rise in her body, she stopped and asked for guidance, for her intuition to lead her in the next direction, the next turn, until she returned to the canyon and the quiet pool.

❖

It was nightfall when the woman climbed down the steep canyon ledges, the child held securely in her arms. When she reached the pool, though there was a cold chill in the air, the woman laid the child's body directly into the quiet water. Gently rippling the surface of the pool, water snakes swam to the girl and with their bodies wove a soft nest for the child to lie on. Fish swam alongside the girl and hugged their fins next to her skin, insulating her body from the chill of the water. Nocturnal animals—bats, owls, raccoons, and nighthawks—

gathered at the edge of the pool or kept vigil overhead in the night sky. The water flowed over the child's wounds, bathing the sores, washing them clean.

"Please be okay," the woman breathed. She knelt at the edge of the pool, hovering over the child. "I do love you. I do. I promise. I promise I'll never leave you again. Come back to me." Hesitantly the woman reached out and touched her hand to the child's head and then to the girl's tiny chest. "Come back to me," she repeated. "Please come back to me."

There was the faintest quiver under her fingertips, a movement so small the woman thought she had imagined it. But then she felt it again.

"Oooh. I can feel it! I can feel your heart beating!" Tears of relief ran down the woman's cheeks.

The child's eyes opened, and her small arms reached

up to the woman. The woman leaned forward, her own tears mixed once again with the water's flow. The little girl clasped her hands around the woman's neck, pulled herself up from the water and into the woman's arms.

CHAPTER EIGHT

hey held each other until the sun rose. The woman could not stop hugging the child. How she loved the softness of her skin and the brightness of her eyes.

"I got you a prize," the little girl finally said.

"Well, thank you," said the woman, "but for the time being, I think I'm going to let go of prizes. Right now I don't need anything else. Having you is the best prize of all."

139

"Well then, it's not a prize," the little girl said. "It's more like a present. I made it for you." Out from under her arm the little girl pulled the cherry-red heart.

"Oh, it's beautiful," the woman said and started to cry again. "I would be so honored to have something that you made."

"It's a little bumpy," the child said and put her hand into the handprint in the middle of the heart. "But I like the color a lot."

"Me, too," said the woman. "I see that you like to make things. I'll remember that."

The woman reached for the gift, and as she did, she felt the place between her breasts begin to ache and grow warm. She took the present from the little girl and held it to the place where her heart had been. A wave of heat swam through her body, from her head to her toes, from her chest to her fingertips. The woman held the present and the little girl even closer. Then the child yawned, rubbed her cheek against the woman's chest, and smiled up at her.

"Can you turn me off now?" the child asked and yawned again. "I've had a busy day."

The woman laughed and kissed the child on the top of her head. "You're right," she said. "It's been quite a day and it *is* time for a rest." The woman took the Universal Remote from her pocket and pushed the button marked "Naptime." The child smiled and disappeared. She left no trace except the felt presence of a handprint on the woman's chest.

When the woman awoke the next morning, the first thing she noticed was a heartbeat inside her chest. Her heart was back! The woman did a jig, turned a cartwheel, leapt into the air—anything to make her heart beat faster, to feel her muscles pulse with the surge of life dancing through her body.

"Now what?" thought the woman. "I've got a heart, but I'm still in the Great Valley." The woman took a deep breath and remembered that her needs had been met in the past and would be again. She remembered that now she had a new way of making decisions.

The woman sat quietly and filled her whole body with breath, nourished each bodily cell before she asked it her question. She spoke first to the child within.

"What do you want?"

The answer came back quickly, simply, "I want to go home." Then she asked her inner self, "Is it time to leave this place or is there more to be learned here?"

The answer came not from her head but from a felt

sense deep within her body: "It's time to leave."

"Then the way will be shown to me," the woman said out loud, and the sense of being guided rather than being in control brought surprising comfort and relief.

The woman did not remember falling asleep, but when she awoke from her brief nap, the Universal Remote blinked beside her with a steady beat. "Direct Flight, Direct Flight," the button read. She pushed the button and immediately left the Great Valley behind. Within seconds she was at the Satellite Conference Center sitting in front of her mentor whose image appeared on a large video screen.

The woman smiled because she could see the look of pleasure on her mentor's face.

"So, uh," the woman stammered with embarrassed pride, "uh . . . that was quite a trip."

Her mentor nodded. "And you did very well."

The woman held up the Universal Remote. "When do I get one of my own?"

Her mentor smiled and answered, "When you have lost as many things as I have and found them all again."

The woman looked down into her lap. The remote had disappeared. She looked back into her mentor's face, knowing that, for now, one part of the journey had been made.

"There is something you will find in your house," the mentor said.

"A surprise?" the woman asked.

"Something you had but have forgotten."

❖

When the woman arrived at her house, it was as if she were entering it for the first time. The rooms were filled with color. The new draperies at her living room window bloomed with bright yellow and red-orange flowers. The new rug in her dining room was a lush, vibrant green. In her bedroom a huge deep cherry-red comforter covered her bed. And plants! There were plants everywhere, filling the large bay window in the dining room, the kitchen window sills, and even hanging beneath the skylight in her bathroom. She would have time to take care of them now.

When the woman walked into her home office, she saw on her computer that she had returned in time for her Face-to-Face meeting. As she reached for the keyboard, something caught her eye. She turned to see the walking stick standing in the corner, its carved head turned toward her. The woman sighed. She felt a deep trust, a sense that she would, in time, know whether her job was the best place for her to be, and that always she would choose those people and those experiences that would bring her closer to herself.

The woman found herself walking upstairs into her attic, remembering how the walking stick had guided her up and down the canyon's ledges. When she reached the last step, the woman turned on a light.

"Strange," she thought to herself, "what did I come up here for?"

Dust particles sparkled in the faint shafts of light streaming from the ceiling's bare light bulb. The woman waited patiently, gazing over tattered boxes and old broken chairs. The smell of the past mixed with the heat of the attic, and the woman waited.

"Oh, yes!" she cried out loud as the realization shot through her body. The woman tore into an old trunk under the slanted roof, flinging books, sweaters, and pillows out onto the floor. There at the bottom of the trunk the woman found what she had been looking for—that first formal photograph of herself as a child. It was just as she had remembered: lace-trimmed dress, bright shiny eyes, and a smile of innocence on the little girl's face.

The woman took the picture down to her bedroom and carefully slid the photograph into the corner of the mirror where every day she could look into the little girl's eyes.

"I'll never forget you again," she said to the child.

The woman ran bath water for a long, warm soak. She put on some quiet music and brewed a cup of her favorite tea.

"La-la-la-li-li," she sang to herself as she stepped into

the steamy tub.

And though, in her life, the woman did have to search for many other things, she never lost her heart again.

❖ ❖ ❖

SUSAN O'HALLORAN

In addition to *The Woman Who Lost Her Heart* and *The Woman Who Found Her Voice*, Susan O'Halloran has authored *Storybook Marriage*, a book of fairy tales for adults, and *The Hunt For Spring*, a picture book for children. She has recorded many of her original tories and songs, including "Growing Up in Chicago," Volumes I and II, and "Mothers and Other Wild Women," with Nancy Donoval and Beth Horner.

While being a mom, Sue has also worked as a dance teacher, disc jockey, television host, corporate scriptwriter, and stand-up comic, and is currently employed as a diversity consultant/facilitator and designer of instructional materials for Bea Young Associates.

As a storyteller, she has performed in many venues, including Chicago's Wild Onion Storytelling Celebration and the National Storytelling Festival's Exchange Place in Jonesborough, Tennessee. She has two grown sons, Terry and Preston Luke, and a granddaughter named Lily Serene. Sue lives in Evanston, Illinois, except in the winter where you can find her in warmer climes.

Susan Delattre has spent much of her working life as an arts educator and performer. She has taught in the Dance Program at the University of Minnesota, has been a member of the Minneapolis women's theater At the Foot of the Mountain, and has done extensive educational work in schools statewide through the Minnesota State Arts Board and the Minnesota Center for Arts Education.

In recent years, Susan has made storytelling a priority through consulting in the workplace and appearing as a storyteller in performance and educational settings. She is currently interested in "informational storytelling," a form that communicates both "hard data" and a larger range of imaginative feeling.

Susan presently follows a lifelong interest in caring for the land through seed-saving, gardening, and working for the development of sustainable agriculture and food systems. She finds peace and renewal in the ancient river valleys and ridges of western Wisconsin.

If you enjoyed *The Woman Who Lost Her Heart,*
you won't want to miss *The Woman Who Found Her Voice!*

by Susan O'Halloran and Susan Delattre

A mystical story of one woman's journey of "howling with the
enemy" to find her true voice. From her magical hawk guide,
she learns to trust the larger web of life;
from a family of wolves, she learns the value of community;
and from a turtle, she discovers the right to *be.*

*"For any woman who has experienced the loss of her own true voice
through grief, betrayal, or fear, this book is a gift."*
—Rebecca D. Armstrong, Director, Joseph Campbell Society

PUBLISHED BY INNISFREE PRESS.

Available from your local bookseller or directly from the publisher (1-800-367-5872).